W9-AJO-223

BERNARD MOST

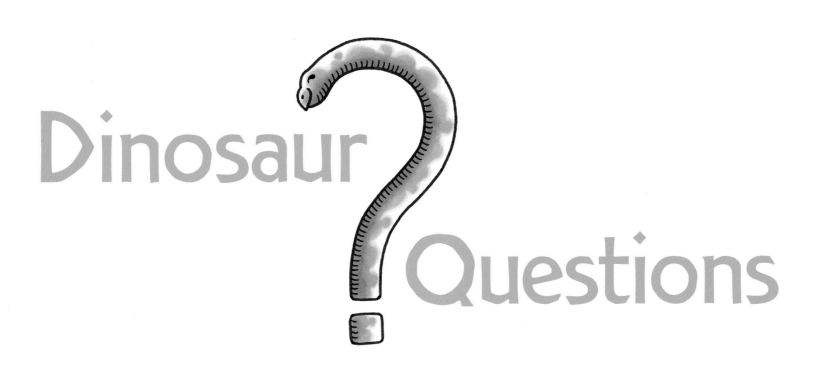

Dinosaur ? Questions

Harcourt Brace & Company

San Diego   New York   London

Library of Congress Cataloging-in-Publication Data
Most, Bernard.
Dinosaur Questions/by Bernard Most. — 1st ed.
p.   cm.
ISBN 0-15-292885-5
1. Dinosaurs — Miscellanea — Juvenile literature. [1. Dinosaurs.
2. Questions and answers.] I. Title.
QE862.D5M6933   1995
567.9'1 — dc20   94-42630

H G F E D C

Printed in Singapore

The illustrations in this book were done in Pantone Tria markers
on Bainbridge board 172, hot-press finish.
The display type was set in Neue Neuland Light by
Photocomposition Center, Harcourt Brace & Company, San Diego, California.
The text type was set in Kabel Book and Kabel Medium by
Thompson Type, San Diego, California.
Color separations by Bright Arts, Ltd., Singapore
Printed and bound by Tien Wah Press, Singapore
This book was printed on totally chlorine-free Nymolla Matte Art paper.
Production supervision by Warren Wallerstein and Kent MacElwee
Designed by Lori J. McThomas

The author wishes to acknowledge the following books as sources
for the factual information contained in the text:
A Field Guide to Dinosaurs by David Lambert
Dinosaur Data Book by David Lambert
The New Illustrated Dinosaur Dictionary by Helen Roney Sattler
Dinosaur Encyclopedia by Donald Lessem and Donald Glut

To Diane D'Andrade,
who wondered whether all the
dinosaur questions had been answered

Whenever I go to a museum and look at dinosaur fossils, or whenever I read a book at the library about dinosaurs, I think of so many dinosaur questions. There are so many things we don't know about dinosaurs. The more I learn about them and the more scientists change their theories about dinosaurs, the more dinosaur questions I have.

What colors were the dinosaurs?

Scientists used to think most dinosaurs were the same color as crocodiles. But they now think some dinosaurs may have had colorful spots, stripes, or patterns like many animals, reptiles, fish, and tropical birds we see today. We'll probably never know what colors the dinosaurs really were. If you could color your own dinosaur, which colors would you choose?

What did dinosaurs eat?

We can guess what a dinosaur ate by studying its mouth and teeth. Sharp, serrated teeth were for tearing meat. Flatter, peglike, and spoon-shaped teeth were for mashing or chewing leaves and twigs. Horny, birdlike beaks were for cropping plants or cracking eggs. Sometimes food fossils are found alongside dinosaur fossils, giving us more clues about dinosaur dinners.

How much did dinosaurs weigh?

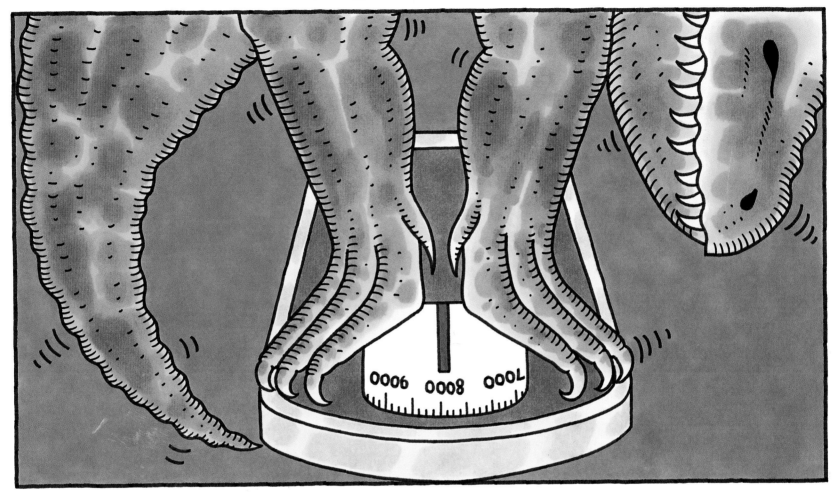

We don't know for sure! Scientists compare body weight, size, and posture of animals like elephants, hippos, and giraffes with dinosaur fossils and use the similarities to guess what dinosaurs might have weighed. Some "guesstimates": Stegosaurus weighed 2 tons, Triceratops weighed 5 tons, Apatosaurus weighed 30 tons, and Seismosaurus may have weighed as much as 100 tons!

What did dinosaurs sound like?

We'll probably never know, but it's fun to guess! Dinosaur fossils show that many dinosaurs could have had vocal structures and could have made sounds. The hollow tubes in the crests of some duck-billed dinosaurs suggest that they made loud, mooselike sounds. What do you think a dinosaur's voice might have sounded like?

How smart were dinosaurs?

Scientists have never found a dinosaur brain, but they can tell brain sizes from skull fossils. They have found that the biggest dinosaurs had the smallest brains. Stegosaurus, who weighed about 2 tons, had a tiny brain the size of a golf ball. Troodon (TROW-a-don), a member of a family of small, agile, two-legged dinosaurs with large brains, is believed to have been the smartest of them all.

Did any dinosaurs give birth to live babies?

Many dinosaur eggs, dinosaur nests, and even dinosaur hatchling fossils have been found. But there is no evidence that dinosaurs gave birth to live young, as mammals do. Since no Apatosaurus eggs have ever been found, some scientists wonder if that dinosaur might have given birth to live babies. Others think ostrichlike dinosaurs, because of their bone structure, might have also given birth to live young.

Were dinosaurs cold-blooded like reptiles . . .

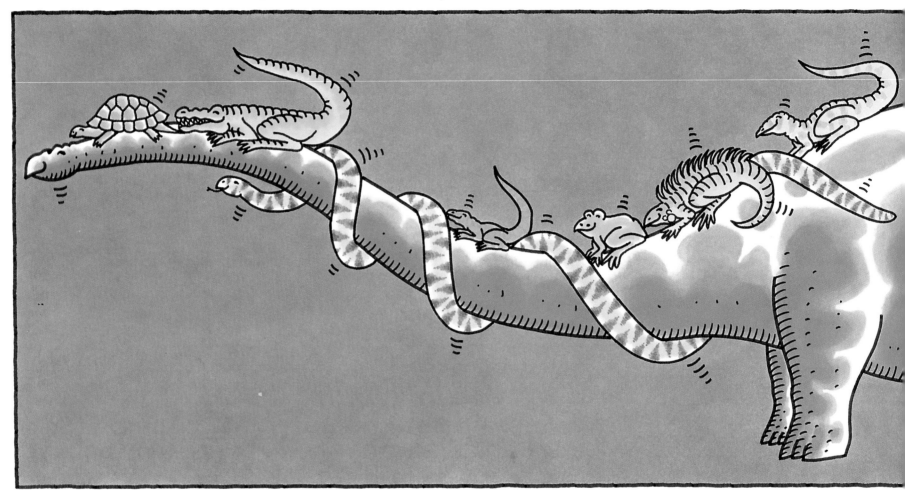

Most cold-blooded animals have lower body temperatures. They cannot control their body temperature, so to keep warm they move into the sun, and to keep cool they move into the shade. To save energy, they move much more slowly than warm-blooded animals. Scientists used to think every dinosaur was cold-blooded. Now, many are changing their theories.

. . . or warm-blooded like birds and mammals?

Warm-blooded animals have higher body temperatures. They have more energy and are more active than cold-blooded animals. Scientists think the large size of some dinosaurs and the plates and fins on other dinosaurs helped control body temperatures. They now think some dinosaurs may have been warm-blooded. Too bad nobody's ever taken a dinosaur's temperature!

Is it Brontosaurus or Apatosaurus?

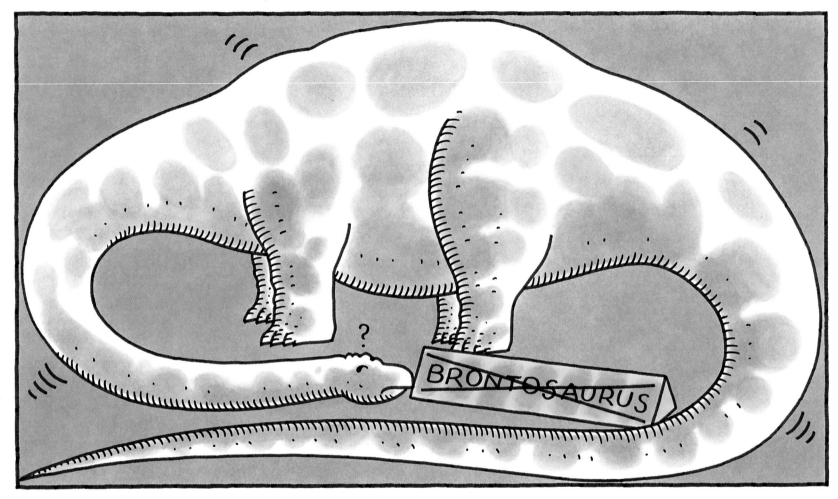

The name of the well-known dinosaur Brontosaurus is a mistake. When Brontosaurus was discovered and named, scientists didn't realize it was the same dinosaur that had been discovered years earlier and named Apatosaurus. The correct scientific name is usually the first one given. But since so many people know this famous dinosaur by its second name, I think they should still call it Brontosaurus!

How can scientists tell if fossils are male or female?

It's not easy to tell the difference! Scientists guess that slimmer, more delicate fossils were female, and the bigger, heavier fossils were male. Based on their knowledge of modern horned animals, they also guess that fossils with bigger facial bumps and horns, or fossils with showy crests were male. But the truth is, we really don't know for sure which is which!

Which dinosaur ran the fastest?

Many dinosaurs were very, very speedy! Tracks of footprints help show us how fast some dinosaurs ran. The ostrichlike dinosaurs were among the fastest dinosaurs. If I had to bet on the speediest dinosaur ever, I would put all my money on Dromiceiomimus (droh-mee-see-a-MY-muss). Experts think it was able to run 40 miles per hour!

Did dinosaurs swim?

Scientists have argued for years over whether dinosaurs could swim. Fossilized footprints have been found that suggest that a four-legged dinosaur's front feet touched the bottom of a lake while its body floated on the surface. Other tracks give clues that two-legged dinosaurs could swim, too. Dinosaurs spent a lot of time near water. Doesn't it make sense that many of them learned how to swim?

Why was one dinosaur named "good mother lizard"?

Among the most amazing dinosaur discoveries are large nests containing many dinosaur babies of different ages. Scientists think these nests were like nurseries because the fossils show that adult dinosaurs brought food to their babies and cared for them. They named this dinosaur Maiasaura (my-a-SAW-ra) because it means "good mother lizard."

Which dinosaur was the biggest?

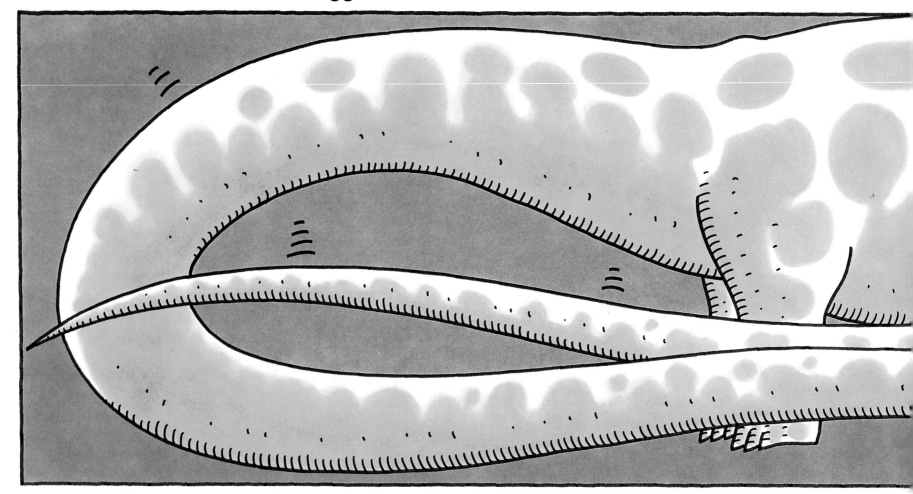

The biggest dinosaur discovered so far is Seismosaurus (size-ma-SAW-russ). It was a four-legged plant eater found in New Mexico. Its bones seem to show that it was 120 to 170 feet long and weighed 80 to 100 tons. This giant dinosaur was almost twice as big and more than twice as heavy as Apatosaurus. That's a lot of dinosaur!

Which dinosaur was the littlest?

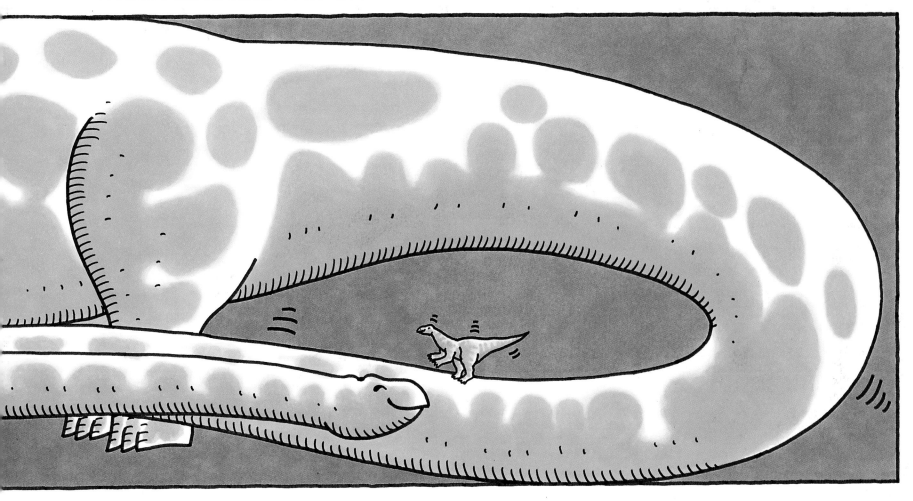

The littlest dinosaur ever discovered is Mussaurus (moo-SAW-russ). Scientists found fossils of a baby mussaurus near a nest in Argentina and nicknamed it "mouse lizard" because it was only 8 inches long. An adult mussaurus would have been about 10 feet long. Do you think the biggest dinosaur would have enjoyed playing with the littlest dinosaur?

Which dinosaur had the longest neck?

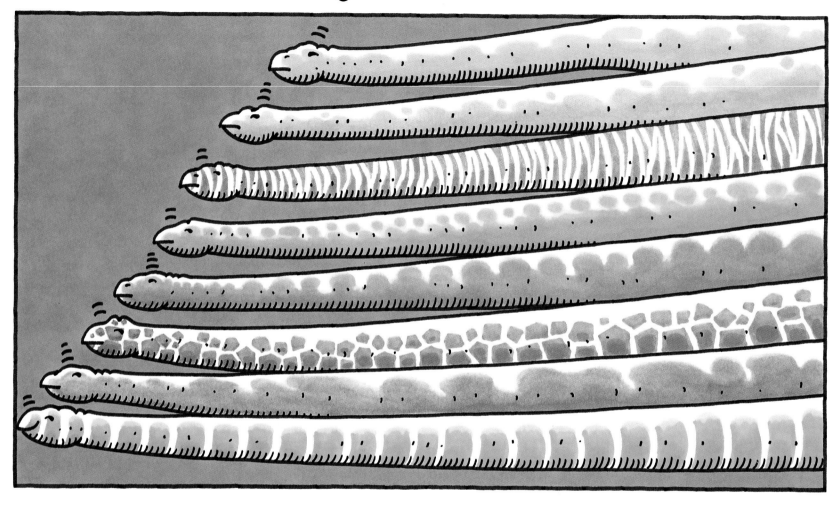

The longest neck of any dinosaur (or for that matter, of any animal that ever lived) belonged to the four-legged plant eater Mamenchisaurus (ma-MEN-chee-saw-russ). Estimates of the length of its neck alone range from 35 to 49 feet. Just imagine how long it took for food to reach this dinosaur's stomach! I wonder if it was always hungry?

Did dinosaurs have ears?

Studies of fossil skulls suggest dinosaurs had internal ears like birds and crocodiles instead of external ears like rabbits and humans. Our knowledge of dinosaurs comes mostly from fossils of their "hard parts," or bones, rarely their "soft parts." We wouldn't know a rabbit had floppy ears, if all we found were its bones. Isn't it possible some dinosaurs had ears like many living animals?

Why is Stegosaurus like a giant dinosaur puzzle?

Stegosaurus was the first dinosaur with plates to be discovered, and experts are still debating how to arrange the plates on Stegosaurus's back. Different arrangements have been tried: A single row of plates from neck to tail; pairs of plates in two rows; plates flopping outward on each side; and the version most experts agree on — two rows of overlapping plates.

Scientists are also still debating what the plates were used for. Were the plates used as armor for protection? Were they used as weapons? As fans for cooling? As solar panels to absorb heat? Were they used to make Stegosaurus appear bigger and more frightening? Or were they used to attract a mate? Isn't Stegosaurus like a giant dinosaur puzzle?

Did some dinosaurs have whiskers?

All we find of many dinosaurs is a single tooth or a few pieces of bone. How do we know dinosaurs didn't have whiskers? There are so many animals living today that have whiskers: cats, mice, rabbits, seals, and walruses. If walrus fossils were found hundreds of thousands of years from now, scientists might not be able to tell if it had whiskers!

Are birds dinosaur cousins?

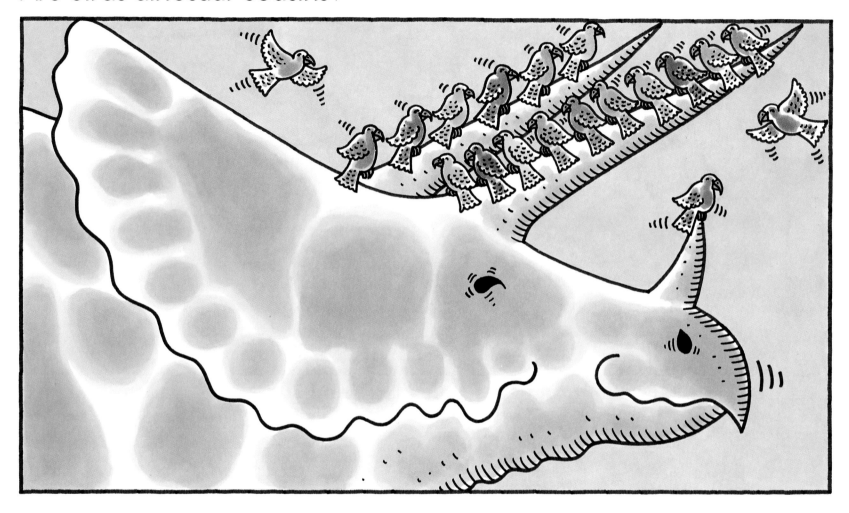

This is one of the biggest dinosaur questions. Many dinosaurs had birdlike necks, birdlike claws, birdlike beaks, and birdlike bone structures. Some dinosaurs built nests and cared for their young. Some may have been warm-blooded like birds, and they may even have had feathers. Many scientists are convinced that birds are dinosaur cousins. What do you think?

How old did dinosaurs grow to be?

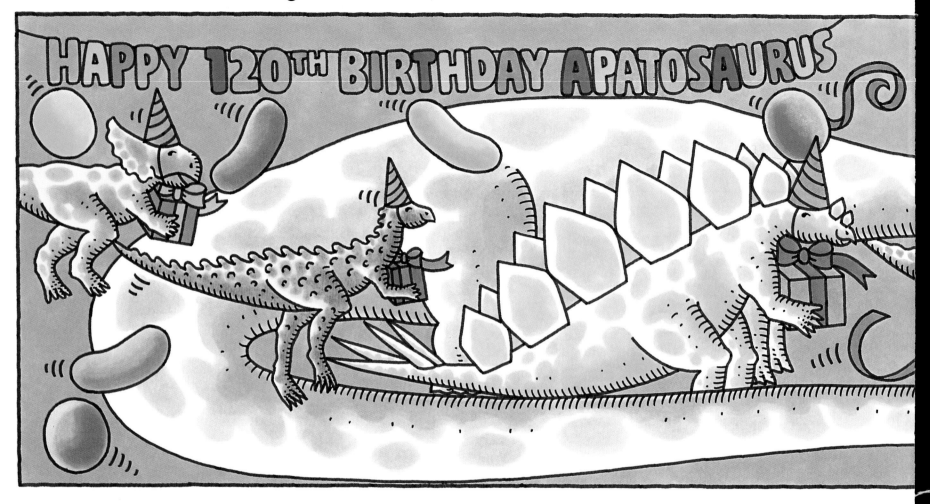

Growth rings in fossil bones suggest that some dinosaurs lived to a ripe old age. Scientists think that if dinosaurs were warm-blooded, they could have lived more than 120 years and if cold-blooded, more than 200 years. But the guess is that most dinosaurs probably died of injury or disease long before they died of old age!

Where is the best place to dig for dinosaurs?

Dinosaur fossils have been found all over the world. They probably lived where you live, but I don't recommend digging up your backyard to search for fossils. Scientists are searching for dinosaur fossils right now, and they say the best places to look are deserts and areas where the soil has been worn away, exposing layers of ancient rock.

Why did dinosaurs disappear?

Did a comet or meteor hit the earth? Did clouds of dust block the sun, destroying the food chain? Did volcanoes cover the earth with volcanic ash, wiping out plant life? Did climate changes make life difficult for dinosaurs? Why didn't crocodiles, lizards, and insects disappear, too? Someday scientists may dig up clues to answer the biggest dinosaur question of all!

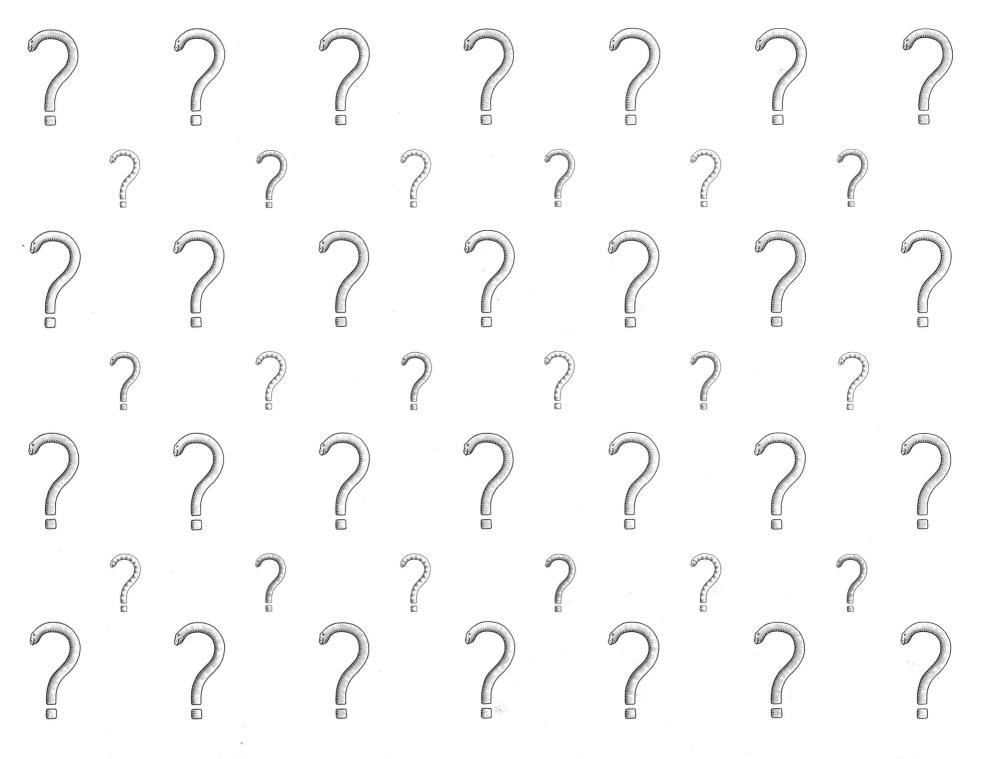